Collins

11+

Verbal Reasoning Vocabulary

Support & Practice Workbook

Chris Pearse, Louise Swann
and Hilary Male

Published by Collins
An imprint of HarperCollins*Publishers* Ltd
1 London Bridge Street
London SE1 9GF

HarperCollins*Publishers*
1st Floor, Watermarque Building, Ringsend Road, Dublin 4, Ireland

ISBN 978-0-00-849739-2

First published 2021

10 9 8 7 6 5 4 3 2 1

British Library Cataloguing in Publication Data.
A CIP record of this book is available from the British Library.
Commissioning: Clare Souza
Authors: Chris Pearse, Louise Swann and Hilary Male
Project Management: Richard Toms and Sundus Pasha
Cover Design: Kevin Robbins and Sarah Duxbury
Inside Concept Design: Ian Wrigley
Typesetting and artwork: Jouve India Private Limited
Production: Karen Nulty

Published in collaboration with Teachitright.
Billy the Bookworm™ is the property of Teachitright Ltd.
Printed and bound in the UK using 100% Renewable Electricity
at CPI Group (UK) Ltd

Contents

Introduction

Teachitright

This book has been published in collaboration with Teachitright, one of the most successful 11+ tuition companies in the South-East. It has supported thousands of pupils for both grammar school and independent school entry. Teachitright has several tuition centres across the UK, including Berkshire, Buckinghamshire and West Midlands.

With considerable experience and knowledge, Teachitright has produced a range of books to support children through their 11+ journey for both CEM style and many Common Entrance exams. The books have been written by qualified teachers, tested in the classroom with pupils and adapted to ensure children are fully prepared and able to perform to the best of their ability.

Teachitright's unique mascot, Billy, helps to guide children through this book and gives helpful hints and tips along the way. We hope your child finds this book useful and informative and we wish them luck on their 11+ journey.

Teachitright hold a number of comprehensive revision courses and mock exams throughout the year. For more information, visit www.teachitright.com

Helping to build your child's future

The Importance of Vocabulary

Vocabulary is a vitally important aspect of all 11+/Common Pre-Test exams. This book contains different verbal reasoning question types to help your child become familiar with the expectations in verbal ability. Teachitright has always recognised the importance of having an extensive word knowledge and how this can impact on other areas of the curriculum. Recording new, unfamiliar words is important for all children to help with revision nearer the exam dates. Also, putting words into context will help them to develop a better understanding of how these words can be used in real-life scenarios.

The book is structured into three key areas:

Learn: In the introduction to each of the lessons, there is a detailed description of the question type and a worked example. This section also provides tips and hints on how to solve the individual question type.

Develop: This section contains 10 questions to help children understand the format and start applying strategies and techniques acquired in the learn section.

An online video tutorial to help with techniques is available at www.collins.co.uk/11plusresources

Timed test: Each lesson ends with 30 questions to practise under timed conditions and enables children to apply the exam techniques taught throughout the lessons.

How to Use this Book

This book provides 10 lessons and these can be followed in order or in isolation. It is important to study the learn sections before attempting the questions, to ensure the correct techniques are applied in the Develop or Timed Test sections. There is a progress chart at the back of the book to help children track their progress. Billy the Bookworm provides supportive statements throughout the book to aid understanding.

LESSON 1:
ODD ONE OUT

Look out for Billy's tips and hints.

LEARN

This question type requires a good understanding of words and is one of the most popular question types used in Verbal Reasoning papers. The main skill you need to have is the ability to group words that are linked or have a similar meaning (synonyms, see Lessons 6 and 7). Furthermore, having a good general knowledge is a useful requirement in these questions. To help develop your understanding of odd one out questions, it can be useful to build word lists around different categories, for example:

- capital cities
- counties
- countries
- young animals
- jobs
- names of sports
- types of flowers and trees
- names of herb and spices

Have a go at placing the following words under the correct headings in the table (you may need to look some of them up in a dictionary):

lacrosse, cygnet, economist, willow, leveret, badminton, sycamore, farmer, kabaddi, fledgling, architect, kid, fencing, oak, chiropractor, yew, farrier, snooker, birch, squeaker

young animals	jobs
trees	**sports**

Let's look at an example.

Three of the words below are linked. Underline the word which is not related to these three.

sphere   cylinder   rhombus   prism

Technique

1. Read all the words given and consider their meanings.

2. Try to group two or three words together that are linked or associated. In the above example you can make a link between *sphere* and *cylinder* as they are both three-dimensional (3D) shapes.

3. Next you can check if *rhombus* or *prism* are 3D shapes. A prism is 3D so can be grouped with *sphere* and *cylinder*.

4. If three words are grouped together, this should leave the word which is the odd one out. In the above example, *rhombus* is the answer as it is the only 2D shape.

Answer: **rhombus**

Another important skill to develop for this question type is having an awareness of words with a dual meaning (homonyms, see Lesson 5).

Let's look at an example.

Three of the words below are linked. Underline the word which is not related to these three.

might   power   strength   maybe

Technique

The first word, *might,* has a double meaning. *Might* can mean strength or the possibility of doing something. Therefore, when grouping *might* with other words it could be paired with *maybe* or *strength* and *power*. As this question type involves grouping three words with an association, it is important to group the correct words together. The Venn diagram below shows how the words can be grouped together as synonyms to leave the odd one out:

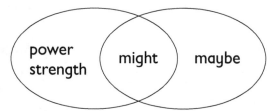

This shows that *might* is the only word which has the same meaning as all the other three words. This helps us deduce that *maybe* is the odd one out because *power, might* and *strength* are the three synonyms.

Answer: **maybe**

DEVELOP

Circle the letter underneath the word which is the odd one out.

1.	thoughtful	kind	caring	interested
	A	B	C	D
2.	mother	aunt	cousin	daughter
	A	B	C	D
3.	tale	report	story	fable
	A	B	C	D
4.	ghost	ghoul	spectre	beast
	A	B	C	D
5.	twinkle	shine	gleam	glow
	A	B	C	D
6.	eagle	hawk	owl	robin
	A	B	C	D
7.	stranger	mate	friend	chum
	A	B	C	D
8.	fringe	middle	edge	boundary
	A	B	C	D
9.	dress	gown	trousers	frock
	A	B	C	D
10.	carrot	potato	swede	peas
	A	B	C	D

Check your answers at the back of the book before moving onto the timed test.

Remember you need to group three words together to leave the odd one out.

TIMED TEST 1

 08:00
08 minutes

Circle the letter underneath the word which is the odd one out.

1.	reprobate	scoundrel	scallywag	donor
	A	B	C	D
2.	slapdash	haphazard	careless	confusing
	A	B	C	D
3.	constant	unchanging	erratic	consistent
	A	B	C	D
4.	pine	elm	beech	oak
	A	B	C	D
5.	Skye	Lundy	Scotland	Jersey
	A	B	C	D
6.	rabbi	sage	imam	priest
	A	B	C	D
7.	persimmon	apricot	blueberry	shallot
	A	B	C	D
8.	waddle	rockhopper	king	emperor
	A	B	C	D
9.	coarse	agreement	uncouth	rude
	A	B	C	D
10.	Siamese	Dalmatian	Persian	Manx
	A	B	C	D
11.	wholeheartedly	fully	somewhat	utterly
	A	B	C	D
12.	malignant	malevolent	mobile	malicious
	A	B	C	D
13.	sever	acute	dire	serious
	A	B	C	D
14.	address	speech	talk	letter
	A	B	C	D

15.	yield	capitulate	force	succumb
	A	B	C	D
16.	happening	scene	occurrence	incident
	A	B	C	D
17.	ruckus	rumpus	hullaballoo	hoard
	A	B	C	D
18.	personable	responsible	amiable	agreeable
	A	B	C	D
19.	perchance	perhaps	particular	maybe
	A	B	C	D
20.	eccentric	idiosyncratic	insane	quirky
	A	B	C	D
21.	intelligible	perplexing	mysterious	bewildering
	A	B	C	D
22.	forthcoming	imminent	distant	impending
	A	B	C	D
23.	curse	jinx	favour	spell
	A	B	C	D
24.	plastic	perspective	stance	view
	A	B	C	D
25.	conduct	music	behaviour	bearing
	A	B	C	D
26.	turmoil	uproar	disconcerted	disruption
	A	B	C	D
27.	inflated	bulbous	overblown	exaggerated
	A	B	C	D
28.	useless	inept	efficacious	ineffectual
	A	B	C	D
29.	sombre	dingy	hat	shady
	A	B	C	D
30.	circuit	fuse	amalgamate	merge
	A	B	C	D

LESSON 2:
ODD TWO OUT

LEARN

The slight variation to the type of question found in Lesson 1 is having to find the **odd two out**. This involves a greater awareness of grouping words with a similar meaning or connection. It is worth noting that the two words which are left over do not always have to be linked to each other. The matching activity below involves making groups of three words from the table which are linked or associated.

Devon	hawk	squash	Yorkshire	Oslo	cricket
linger	ruby	osprey	eagle	emerald	loiter
snooker	dawdle	sapphire	Helsinki	Rome	Cornwall

Group 1: _____   _____   _____

Group 2: _____   _____   _____

Group 3: _____   _____   _____

Group 4: _____   _____   _____

Group 5: _____   _____   _____

Group 6: _____   _____   _____

Thinking of different words that belong in a category can be a good exercise to help you with this question type. Ask your parents or guardian to suggest a category and try to think of as many words as possible that belong in that group. Here are some to get you started.

- fruit and vegetables
- capital cities
- countries in Africa or Europe
- big cats
- animals with four legs
- jobs

This could easily be turned into a game, with points awarded for the most words in that category.

DEVELOP

Find the two words which are different from the others. Circle the two answers.

1.	hands	minutes	horse	seconds	hours
	A	B	C	D	E
2.	thought	between	inside	because	within
	A	B	C	D	E
3.	mauve	cerise	rose	violet	salmon
	A	B	C	D	E
4.	cheese	beef	pork	butter	lamb
	A	B	C	D	E
5.	relax	cold	icy	rest	freezing
	A	B	C	D	E
6.	father	uncle	son	cousin	sibling
	A	B	C	D	E
7.	lounge	kitchen	shed	bathroom	garage
	A	B	C	D	E
8.	centipede	butterfly	bumblebee	earwig	spider
	A	B	C	D	E
9.	inspire	motivate	expire	encourage	lapse
	A	B	C	D	E
10.	enjoy	abhor	relish	dislike	appreciate
	A	B	C	D	E

Check your answers at the back of the book before moving onto the timed test.

TIMED TEST 2

08:00
08 minutes

Circle the letters underneath the words which are the two odd ones out.

1.	cabbage	potato	lettuce	carrot	spinach
	A	B	C	D	E
2.	book	magazine	newspaper	library	newsagent
	A	B	C	D	E
3.	rug	carpet	door	mat	floor
	A	B	C	D	E
4.	rose	lemon	mint	lily	daisy
	A	B	C	D	E
5.	shock	embark	start	begin	aboard
	A	B	C	D	E
6.	cockle	strength	limpet	cheerful	mussel
	A	B	C	D	E
7.	emu	blackbird	penguin	robin	sparrow
	A	B	C	D	E
8.	mission	assignment	expedition	camp	holiday
	A	B	C	D	E
9.	buried	underground	secret	treasure	subterranean
	A	B	C	D	E
10.	expel	inject	discharge	eject	expect
	A	B	C	D	E
11.	cease	converse	conclude	concede	finish
	A	B	C	D	E
12.	gap	puncture	hole	perforate	rupture
	A	B	C	D	E
13.	flourish	disappear	shrink	shrivel	wither
	A	B	C	D	E
14.	begin	dance	think	happy	table
	A	B	C	D	E

15.	child	companion	friend	ally	person
	A	B	C	D	E
16.	great	good	grate	hearth	chimney
	A	B	C	D	E
17.	prominent	outstanding	protruding	intruding	ingrowing
	A	B	C	D	E
18.	ramble	wander	stroll	bramble	marathon
	A	B	C	D	E
19.	whisper	sermon	instruct	lecture	speech
	A	B	C	D	E
20.	daisy	mint	tulip	sage	rose
	A	B	C	D	E
21.	hope	faith	mercy	greed	jealousy
	A	B	C	D	E
22.	fox	artful	crafty	cunning	artwork
	A	B	C	D	E
23.	sow	foal	mare	bullock	ewe
	A	B	C	D	E
24.	abandon	abode	habitat	dwelling	building
	A	B	C	D	E
25.	brisk	rapid	quick	steady	sedate
	A	B	C	D	E
26.	relay	baton	communicate	transmit	race
	A	B	C	D	E
27.	fragment	block	splinter	paper	scrap
	A	B	C	D	E
28.	madam	rotor	think	kayak	look
	A	B	C	D	E
29.	idle	idol	sluggish	indolent	speedy
	A	B	C	D	E
30.	quell	fire	dragon	extinguish	allay
	A	B	C	D	E

**THIS PAGE HAS DELIBERATELY
BEEN LEFT BLANK**

LESSON 3:
RESHUFFLED SENTENCES

LEARN

This question type involves reordering a muddled sentence and finding one word which is superfluous to the others (that is, a word that is not needed to complete the sentence). To do this, you need to understand how a sentence is constructed and which words are more likely to be placed together to make grammatical sense. An important skill is being able to identify which words belong to particular word classes.

In the mixed-up sentence below, can you match the words to the correct word class by drawing lines?

in enjoy I looking gallery the art antique pictures at

verb	pronoun	noun	article	adjective	preposition

Sentences often start with a pronoun or a subordinating conjunction and may be followed by a verb. All sentences must contain a theme and a verb.

Pronouns might include:	**Here are some common subordinating conjunctions:**
I, you, he, she, it, we, they	after, although, as, before, how, if, once, since, though, until, when, where, whether, while

So, if we look at the sentence above we can recognise the pronoun 'I' and the verb 'enjoy'. This starts the sentence 'I enjoy . . .'. The next question to ask yourself is, what is being enjoyed? This forms the theme of the sentence and this would be '. . . looking at antique pictures'. Lastly, the words remaining indicate the location.

I enjoy looking at antique pictures in the art gallery.

Let's look at an example.

<u>Underline</u> the word which is superfluous to the sentence.

some want to sport for go I have time

I want to have some time for sport.

Technique

1. Read the sentence as it is written and consider what would make sense. Often this will help you understand the context of the sentence.

2. Look for the pronoun or subordinating conjunction as this may start the sentence. This word will often be followed by the verb. In the above example the word 'I' can help begin the sentence.

3. Once you start the sentence you can cross out the words used and this will help leave the omitted word. If two words are left over, you need to think about where one of the words might fit in the sentence. For example, it might be an adjective to describe one of the words you already have in the sentence.

4. Double check that the sentence makes sense.

Answer: **go**

DEVELOP

Underline the word which is superfluous to the sentence.

1. cooked after she it court fish the caught he

2. nobody else likes hurting to somebody hurt

3. new by door is house close the very

4. a I quacking chorus of quaking ducks heard

5. we strike won quite match easily the

6. is it everyone for fun yesterday was such

7. shopping birthday mother's was gone his for present has he

8. can closer far so see I move you

9. was he determine on well doing intent

10. must precisely regulations behind follow you the

Check your answers at the back of the book before moving onto the timed test.

TIMED TEST 3

15:00
15 minutes

Underline the word which is superfluous to the sentence.

1. weather she under today umbrella is feeling the

2. continue our should as we plans think I with

3. know of don't think I myself stupid as

4. is need that really there a for honest

5. are dusk we fly plane due at to

6. special he on occasions is invited in not

7. her hand great held he esteem in

8. journey a arduous the long is one difficulty and

9. cold was during the library extremely it in

10. going road you when are the do crossing not run

11. burst when clown laughing everyone out him they saw

12. walk the enjoyed we because despite rain the

13. got bed climbed into snuggles and stairs James the

14. arrive a museum Saturday we the visited afternoon on

15. concerned might himself that they I he hurt am

16. hair brush morning shampoo mirror I and my every

17. don't problem it understand quite your I

18. going not plan unable to without a we succeed are

19. he cutting scissors made very remark a

20. shoes mistake by her right left she

21. Thursday I dancing every day on a week go

22. I was forward looking a time having down wonderful to

23. dog speed after the raced stick the quick

24. successfully secret was agent accomplished mission the

25. unfortunately not preference was my available choose first

26. I problem I think know where down the lies

27. temperatures disruption caused the led winter services extreme to

28. fix to repaired Dad to ought able it be

29. he skilled swerving famous was ball at the extremely

30. inclined slope was to not he answer

Eliminating the words used can help identify the word which is superfluous.

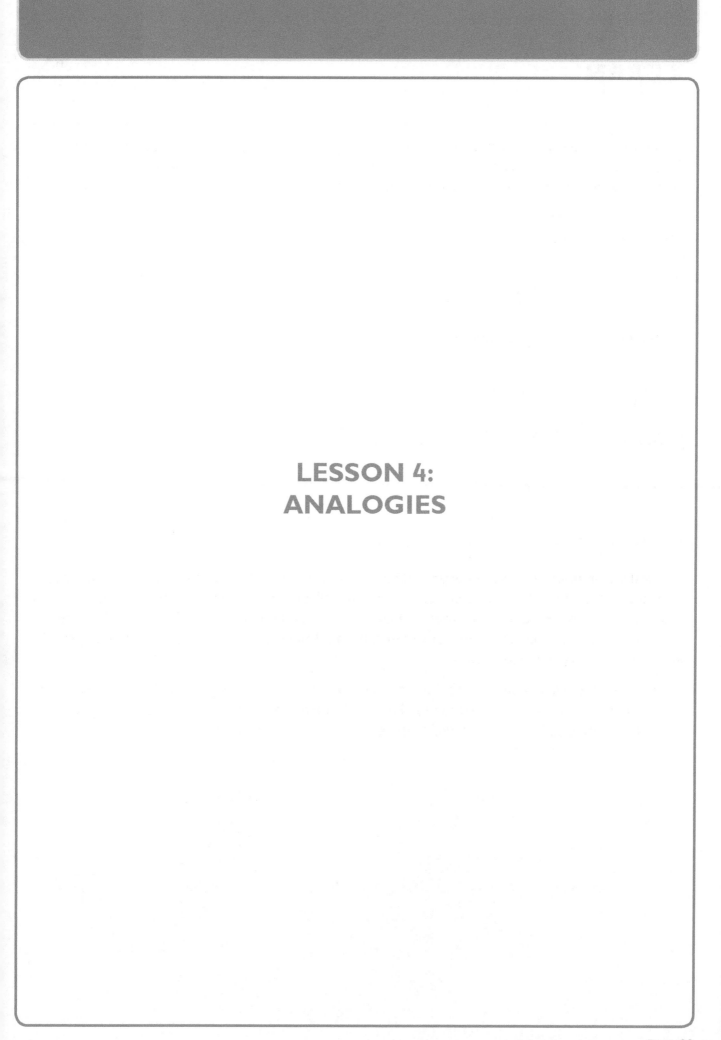

LESSON 4:
ANALOGIES

LEARN

Being able to recognise an analogy relies on being able to compare one thing with another. Analogy actually means similarity, and this question type often involves good general knowledge and making logical links between words.

Below are some incomplete analogies. Can you place a word at the end of each analogy to help it make a sensible sentence?

Cat is to kitten as dog is to _____.

Architect is to drawings as author is to _____.

Emerald is to green as ruby is to _____.

Radius is to arm as fibula is to _____.

Loop is to pool as keep is to _____.

Loathe is to hate as adore is to _____.

You must remember in these questions, that the link between the second pair of words must be the same as the link in the first pair. So, it is useful to consider how the words might be related. There are a number of ways in which words can be connected. For example, they could be associated by synonyms, antonyms, homophones, jobs, colours, cities, backward spellings or parts of our bodies.

Sometimes the link will be very obvious and can be spotted instantly. On other questions, you might need to consider what every word means before the link becomes evident. Saying the completed analogy in your mind will help reinforce the correct answer.

Let's look at an example.

Grate is to (great, cheese, fire) **as peal is to** (slice, peel, knife).

Technique

1. Read the words in the analogy and think about the link between the first pair of words. In the above example the words *grate* and *great* are homophones. (A homophone refers to two or more words that have the same pronunciation but different meanings or spellings). If this link is spotted quickly it can be applied to the second pair of words.

2. Establish a connection between the first pair of words and decide which word will make the same link between the second pair of words.

3. Ruling out words and eliminating them can help limit your choices.

4. Double check that the analogy makes sense and there is verb agreement.

Answer: great, peel

DEVELOP

Underline **one** word from each set of brackets to best complete the analogy.

1. Kitten is to (cat, fur, bark) as puppy is to (dog, animal, mammal).

2. Paper is to (pencil, book, library) as glass is to (cup, window, wine).

3. Water is to (snow, liquid, rain) as ice is to (snowman, solid, melt).

4. Train is to (station, rails, ticket) as car is to (petrol, traffic, road).

5. Dance is to (feet, shoe, hop) as clap is to (cheer, hands, applause).

6. Truth is to (obey, honesty, fiction) as lying is to (villain, deceit, distrust).

7. Happiness is to (laugh, smile, joy) as anger is to (sorrow, frown, cry).

8. Shoe is to (foot, laces, socks) as trousers are to (pocket, belt, jeans).

9. Sight is to (eyes, visible, see) as hearing is to (audible, deaf, ears).

10. Sweet is to (sugar, candy, charming) as savoury is to (dinner, meal, salt).

Check your answers at the back of the book before moving onto the timed test.

TIMED TEST 4

15:00
15 minutes

<u>Underline</u> **one** word from each set of brackets to best complete the analogy.

1. Narrow is to (alley, confined, squeeze) as wide is to (spacious, large, plain).

2. Vacate is to (engage, room, empty) as occupy is to (fill, vacant, burst).

3. Jovial is to (cheerful, happily, dance) as gloomy is to (dark, despondent, cry).

4. Renowned is to (famous, queen, star) as obscure is to (infamous, forgotten, unknown).

5. Porous is to (sponge, cup, lake) as waterproof is to (rubber, boots, bucket).

6. Forego is to (diet, deny, without) as indulge is to (binge, want, require).

7. Wan is to (sick, lazy, plain) as glowing is to (exercise, healthy, smile).

8. Denial is to (argument, agree, contradiction) as agreement is to (confirmation, truth, disagree).

9. Barren is to (fall, wither, unproductive) as fertile is to (grow, fruitful, bushy).

10. Irritation is to (annoy, exasperation, frustrate) as appreciation is to (value, happy, lovely).

11. Novice is to (expert, nun, amateur) as freshman is to (expert, graduate, professional).

12. Cherry is to (stone, red, blossom) as apple is to (tree, pip, delicious).

13. Noble is to (true, title, wealth) as humble is to (glad, poverty, simple).

14. Chick is to (cheep, cheap, squeak) as duck is to (egg, quack, quake).

15. Spontaneous is to (fast, impromptu, sudden) as prepared is to (review, rehearsed, practice).

16. Snout is to (boar, bore, tail) as trunk is to (elephant, suitcase, safari).

17. Strange is to (natural, bizarre, bazaar) as familiar is to (like, ordinary, odd).

18. Rabbit is to (hairy, bun, hare) as wallaby is to (Australian, marsupial, kangaroo).

19. Foot is to (heal, heel, ankle) as hand is to (palm, finger, wrist).

20. Gallop is to (hoarse, horse, hound) as slither is to (snake, fish, lizard).

21. Elver is to (salmon, eel, cod) as joey is to (possum, partridge, kiwi).

22. Five is to (twenty-five, fifty, fifteen) as two is to (four, twelve, three).

23. Miner is to (pit, coal, lamp) as brewer is to (beer, keg, pint).

24. Portrait is to (art, brush, painter) as statue is to (sculptor, builder, stone).

25. War is to (battle, raw, mud) as smart is to (bus, car, trams).

26. Composer is to (notes, music, instrument) as philosopher is to (library, brain, ideas).

27. Forty-eight is to (eight, four, nine) as twenty-four is to (five, four, eight).

28. Knits is to (knitter, stink, socks) as straw is to (hay, hair, warts).

29. Deer is to (fawn, cub, pup) as pigeon is to (chicken, fledgling, squab).

30. Astronomer is to (rocket, space, atmosphere) as meteorologist is to (weather, meteors, rain).

The relationship between both pairs of words must be the same.

LESSON 5:
MULTIPLE MEANINGS

LEARN

Having a good grasp of homonyms is important in this question type. Homonyms are words that are both spelt and often pronounced the same, but have different meanings. The main skill involved in these questions is knowing the multiple meanings of the word, so, to help you practise this skill, some homonyms are listed below for you to define. The first one has been done for you.

Word	Definition
bow	To bend your head or body forward, especially as a way of showing someone respect or expressing thanks to people who have watched you perform
bow	A knot with two curved parts and two loose ends, used as a decoration or to tie shoes
close	
close	
badger	
badger	
dear	
dear	
sow	
sow	
wind	
wind	
kind	
kind	
court	
court	

Often the most common meanings of a word are known, but it is worth learning the more unusual definitions. For example, the word *bore* we know to mean how something that is not very interesting makes us feel, but you can also *bore* a hole into the ground. Why not use a dictionary to check the different meanings and then keep a record of these definitions so you can revise them before your exams?

Let's look at an example.

Circle the letter of the word that means the same as all the words in brackets.

(message, letter)			(tone, sound)	
memo	sign	record	note	entry
A	**B**	**C**	**D**	**E**

Technique

1. Read the words in the brackets and think about their meanings. Sometimes it can be easier to focus on one word from each set of brackets if the second word is more complex.

2. Look at the five options and consider if any have the same meaning as both sets of words in brackets. In the above example, *memo* could be linked with message and letter but it doesn't mean tone or sound.

3. Ruling out words and eliminating them can help limit your choices.

4. Double check that the word you have chosen links with both sets of brackets. You can do this by putting your answer into a sentence and substituting the words in one set of brackets. Repeat this process for the other set of words in brackets.

Answer: **note**

DEVELOP

Circle the letter underneath the word which best fits both sets of brackets.

1.
(fruit, palm)			**(day, occasion)**	
nut	week	weak	celebration	date
A	B	C	D	E

2.
(departs, exits)			**(foliage, needles)**	
goodbye	leaves	fronds	journey	embark
A	B	C	D	E

3.
(direct, guide)			**(tip, summit)**	
point	apex	aim	top	score
A	B	C	D	E

4.
(fair, just)			**(clockwise, dextral)**	
left	light	right	allow	privilege
A	B	C	D	E

5.
(print, lettering)			**(kind, category)**	
class	variety	write	type	sort
A	B	C	D	E

6.
(ascended, climbed)			**(pink, blush)**	
rise	rose	sunset	flower	redden
A	B	C	D	E

7.
(loop, knot)			**(bob, curtsy)**	
arrow	tie	bend	bow	greet
A	B	C	D	E

8. **(twisted, wrapped)**   **(injure, insult)**

string	hurt	wound	round	offend
A	B	C	D	E

9. **(time, moment)**   **(small, miniscule)**

minute	mind	our	hour	microscope
A	B	C	D	E

10. **(seamstress, tailor)**   **(drain, gutter)**

cloth	sow	sew	gush	sewer
A	B	C	D	E

Check your answers at the back of the book before moving onto the timed test.

The word selected must mean the same as both sets of words in brackets.

TIMED TEST 5

Circle the letter underneath the word which best fits both sets of brackets.

1.
	(carry, lift)		**(teddy, polar)**	
bring	bare	bear	toy	child
A	B	C	D	E

2.
	(hoop, loop)		**(sound, bell)**	
sing	dance	ring	circle	court
A	B	C	D	E

3.
	(stick, racket)		**(rodent, vampire)**	
ball	mouse	court	cricket	bat
A	B	C	D	E

4.
	(solitary, only)		**(foot, shoe)**	
soul	sole	heel	single	sock
A	B	C	D	E

5.
	(clever, smart)		**(beaming, shining)**	
vivid	rich	flashing	bright	glad
A	B	C	D	E

6.
	(alright, okay)		**(thin, wispy)**	
delicate	prime	fine	clear	rare
A	B	C	D	E

7.
	(lord, lady)		**(peep, look)**	
peek	peak	knight	night	peer
A	B	C	D	E

8.

	(floor, earth)		**(minced, crushed)**	
mud	coffee	soil	ground	grind
A	B	C	D	E

9.

	(nice, good)		**(sort, type)**	
kind	alike	honourable	bad	letter
A	B	C	D	E

10.

	(blow, gale)		**(meander, loop)**	
breeze	hurricane	wind	fiver	water
A	B	C	D	E

11.

	(illuminate, brighten)		**(weightless, flimsy)**	
light	bright	heavy	lamp	weigh
A	B	C	D	E

12.

	(contest, fixture)		**(taper, lighter)**	
compete	candle	match	game	play
A	B	C	D	E

13.

	(clasp, catch)		**(trim, cut)**	
buckle	clip	zip	scissors	hold
A	B	C	D	E

14.

	(shove, push)		**(trawler, liner)**	
pull	tug	barge	boat	ferry
A	B	C	D	E

15.

	(shout, yelp)		**(cork, rind)**	
play	yell	stone	fear	bark
A	B	C	D	E

16.

	(sterling, money)		**(beat, pummel)**	
penny	hit	pence	pound	push
A	B	C	D	E

17.

	(well, healthy)		**(position, insert)**	
fit	but	ill	furnish	endow
A	B	C	D	E

18.

	(line, column)		**(fight, squabble)**	
agree	scold	row	tier	queue
A	B	C	D	E

19.

	(gap, area)		**(cosmos, universe)**	
space	planet	volume	infinite	order
A	B	C	D	E

20.

	(locomotive, tube)		**(practise, improve)**	
rehearse	exercise	train	passenger	holiday
A	B	C	D	E

21.

	(healthy, thriving)		**(spring, fount)**	
fit	well	grow	waterfall	pool
A	B	C	D	E

22.

	(leave, flee)		**(wasteland, wilderness)**	
dessert	disappear	wild	desert	fast
A	B	C	D	E

23.

	(cry, drop)		**(rip, shred)**	
tear	dew	salty	rent	slash
A	B	C	D	E

24.   **(festival, fete)**   **(just, equitable)**

honest	fun	fair	fare	equal
A	B	C	D	E

25.   **(abandoned, vacated)**   **(port, sinistral)**

gone	starboard	leave	left	live
A	B	C	D	E

26.   **(bomb, explosive)**   **(pit, colliery)**

mine	dig	blast	quarry	ours
A	B	C	D	E

27.   **(plank, branch)**   **(journal, record)**

diary	log	page	tree	twig
A	B	C	D	E

28.   **(tire, exhaust)**   **(drill, perforate)**

boar	tedious	hole	bore	whole
A	B	C	D	E

29.   **(booth, kiosk)**   **(stop, delay)**

brake	break	stall	shed	cancel
A	B	C	D	E

30.   **(gesture, signal)**   **(breaker, ripple)**

surf	wave	flag	flutter	flood
A	B	C	D	E

THIS PAGE HAS DELIBERATELY BEEN LEFT BLANK

LESSON 6:
MATCHING SYNONYMS

LEARN

In most Verbal Reasoning tests you will be given questions which test a knowledge of words with a similar meaning (synonyms). To help build a good understanding of synonyms, there are a variety of games and activities that you can play. A very simple pencil and paper game is recording as many words with the same meaning as possible. This paired or family activity is outlined below.

The word chosen is fast.

Player 1	Player 2
brisk	rapid
quick	speedy
nimble	lively
flying	express

This game is continued until one player can't think of any more synonyms. After the game has finished it can be useful to look up the starting word in a thesaurus or a synonyms/ antonyms dictionary to find any other synonyms which could have been used. Putting the word into context will also help you retain the meaning, for example a fast sports car or a brisk sports car.

Often flashcards can be used to learn synonyms and they can also help to keep track of words learnt. The important aspect of developing a good knowledge of synonyms is repeating the words until they are embedded and making the quantity of words manageable to practise.

Let's look at an example.

Choose a word from the group to match the word in bold on the left.

foliage   lattice   leaves   station   follow

Technique

1. Read the word on the left and consider the meaning. Sometimes making the word on the left an easier word can help identify the synonym. For example *foliage* might be converted to *vegetation*.

2. Look at the four option words and consider whether they have the same meaning as the word on the left.

3. Ruling out words and eliminating them can help limit your choices. In the above example *station, lattice* and *follow* have no association or link with *foliage*. In synonym questions, they often hide antonyms to try to confuse you. Do not be tricked!

4. Double check that the words mean the same. This can easily be checked by putting the words into the same sentence.

Answer: **leaves**

DEVELOP

Choose a word from the group to match the word on the left. Circle the correct letter underneath the word.

1. **write**

scribble	author	paper	crayon
A	B	C	D

2. **glad**

miserable	glum	pleased	sob
A	B	C	D

3. **cast**

throw	players	catch	clutch
A	B	C	D

4. **boast**

boost	blush	bring	brag
A	B	C	D

5. **factory**

mall	mill	office	building
A	B	C	D

6. **reply**

retort	replace	repeat	boom
A	B	C	D

7. **stretch**

contract	expand	tract	elastic
A	B	C	D

8. **check**

respect	leave	kerb	examine
A	B	C	D

9. **novice**

train	expert	learner	veteran
A	B	C	D

10. **positively**

purely	possibly	definitely	potentially
A	B	C	D

Check your answers at the back of the book before moving onto the timed test.

TIMED TEST 6

15:00
15 minutes

Choose a word to match the meaning of the word on the left. Circle the correct letter underneath the word.

1.	**idol**	idle A	icon B	tyrant C	fame D
2.	**sketch**	crayon A	paper B	design C	canvas D
3.	**plump**	slender A	stout B	thin C	plush D
4.	**mend**	restore A	break B	mould C	touch D
5.	**lament**	celebrate A	weep B	chuckle C	weave D
6.	**lagoon**	stream A	river B	bank C	reservoir D
7.	**hopeful**	discouraging A	optimistic B	honour C	keep D
8.	**robust**	brittle A	secured B	tired C	sturdy D
9.	**copious**	scarce A	scary B	ample C	minimal D
10.	**beg**	plead A	return B	borrow C	force D
11.	**hike**	trek A	reduce B	descend C	run D
12.	**bleak**	lush A	full B	bare C	light D
13.	**giggle**	chortle A	giddy B	smile C	snivel D
14.	**sly**	trick A	brave B	open C	crafty D

15.	umpire	assistant A	referee B	civilised C	ultimate D
16.	neutral	biased A	impartial B	partisan C	nervous D
17.	massive	minute A	master B	mammoth C	mountains D
18.	jostle	push A	pull B	join C	fright D
19.	expose	hidden A	cover B	protect C	reveal D
20.	dent	uneven A	depression B	gloom C	crater D
21.	companion	stranger A	company B	chum C	squad D
22.	bench	table A	basket B	strip C	pew D
23.	amend	swap A	edit B	keep C	adaptor D
24.	cease	halt A	proceed B	bring C	start D
25.	intrusion	liberation A	prohibit B	trespass C	hostage D
26.	mandatory	mandate A	oblige B	optional C	compulsory D
27.	notion	idea A	record B	nought C	present D
28.	parallel	divergence A	aligned B	different C	allegory D
29.	worker	factory A	hard-working B	employer C	operative D
30.	yearn	longer A	favour B	yarn C	hanker D

LESSON 7:
SYNONYMS – INSERT THE LETTERS

LEARN

There are different ways of presenting synonym questions. This next question type relies on a good knowledge of words that are similar in meaning and also on being a good speller. To help introduce this question type, here are a few words that are synonym anagrams of the word on the left.

Word	Anagram (synonym)	Unjumbled
Example: dry	rida	arid
1. cross	gryna	_____
2. hide	oncelca	_____
3. brook	tresam	_____
4. gifted	detalnet	_____
5. supervise	cwtah	_____
6. sorrow	riegf	_____
7. fire	scka	_____

It is important to realise in this type of question that the answer must be in the same word class as the word on the left. For example, if the word on the left is a verb, the answer must also be a verb.

There are plenty of excellent word games that can help improve your spellings. Bananagrams® is a very popular game and old classics like Scrabble™ can also enhance spelling skills. Boggle® is another fun game to help you identify how words are formed.

Let's look at an example.

Complete the word on the right to spell a word that is a synonym of the word on the left.

grave   __er__ous

Technique

1. Read the word on the left and consider its meaning. Look at the incomplete word to see if the letters provided give a clue to the word needed.

2. Inserting possible vowels or consonants which could belong in the spaces can also help identify the word.

3. Thinking about common letter strings can also help with this question type. This could be prefixes and suffixes. In the above example *-ous* is a common suffix.

4. Double check that the words mean the same. This can be easily checked by putting the words into the same sentence.

5. Blend together the letters that you have to hear the sounds (graphemes) that they make. This might help you to hear an appropriate word.

Answer: **serious**

DEVELOP

Insert the missing letters.

1. shout   s __ __ e a __

2. gifted   t __ l __ __ t e __

3. cupboard   __ __ b i n __ t

4. rain   d __ __ z __ l e

5. rotate   s __ __ n

6. stale   __ o u l __ __

7. true   c o __ __ e c __

8. wander   s __ __ o l __

9. hate   __ i s l __ __ __

10. evening   t __ __ __ __ g h t

Check your answers at the back of the book before moving onto the timed test.

TIMED TEST 7

15:00
15 minutes

Insert the missing letters.

1.   ample   e n __ __ __ h

2.   delighted   e c __ __ __ t i c

3.   occupation   p r __ f e s s __ __ __

4.   luxurious   e x __ __ __ v a g a n t

5.   fleeting   m o m e __ t __ __ __

6.   picturesque   a t t __ __ __ t __ v e

7.   irresponsible   __ a r e l __ __ __

8.   modest   h __ __ __ l e

9.   hazardous   __ e r i l __ __ __

10. lightweight   f __ __ __ s y

11. tedious   b __ r __ __ __

12. tease   r i d __ __ __ l e

13. irregular   c __ __ __ k e d

14. naive   g u __ __ __ b l e

15. magnify   e n l __ __ __ e

16.	quantity	__ m o u __ __
17.	narrate	d e s __ __ __ b e
18.	anonymous	__ __ n a m __ d
19.	pamphlet	l __ __ f __ __ t
20.	attract	e n __ __ __ e
21.	tranquil	p __ __ c e __ __ __
22.	bravery	c __ __ r a g __
23.	significant	s __ z e __ b l __
24.	hoist	r a i __ __
25.	permit	l i c e __ __ __
26.	tasty	d e l __ __ __ o u s
27.	praise	c o m p __ __ __ e n t
28.	assembly	g a __ __ e r __ __ g
29.	apathetic	u n __ __ t e __ e s t __ __
30.	company	__ u s __ __ e s s

Using the letters provided to give a clue to the word can help. Also, look at the suffixes and prefixes.

LESSON 8:
MATCHING ANTONYMS

LEARN

This lesson returns to focusing on antonyms but the question type is presented slightly differently. The option words are provided and you must select the correct word from the list given that is opposite to the word on the left-hand side.

To help develop your knowledge of opposites, see if you can match the words in the table below that are antonyms.

split	dismount	rude	cheap	frown	furious
eerie	hinder	combine	raise	risky	mount
content	demolish	dear	lead	polite	aid
lower	smile	safe	bright	build	follow

1. _____ _____   7. _____ _____

2. _____ _____   8. _____ _____

3. _____ _____   9. _____ _____

4. _____ _____   10. _____ _____

5. _____ _____   11. _____ _____

6. _____ _____   12. _____ _____

It is important to realise that some words can belong to more than one word group. For example, in the table above you will have noticed the word *dear*. This can be an endearing (kind) word to say to somebody. For example, 'My *dear* little granddaughter wrote me a lovely letter' said the old lady. The other meaning of dear is 'expensive' and might be mentioned in a shop if an object is costly. This knowledge of words with dual meaning is also focused on in Lesson 5.

In these questions you can also apply elimination to help limit your choices. This simple method also ensures you have checked every word and not jumped to the wrong conclusion. Remember, accuracy is more important than speed.

Let's look at an example.

Select a word from the right that is opposite in meaning to the word on the left.

varied   diverse   different   preferable   constant

Technique

1. Read the word on the left and think about its meaning and a possible antonym. Sometimes simplifying the word on the left will help. In the example above, if you changed the word *varied* to *different* this might make finding the antonym easier.

2. Look at the option words and think about their meanings. Can you rule out any of the words which are synonyms to the word on the left? If so, cross these out. In the above example both *diverse* and *different* are synonyms.

3. If time allows, putting the word into a sentence can help you establish if the words are antonyms. In the above example you could use the first word and then try swapping in the second word to see if the sentence means the opposite. For example:

    The weather always seems to be *varied* in Britain.

    The weather always seems to be *constant* in Britain.

4. Double check that the word is the opposite in meaning and that you haven't chosen a synonym – that mistake is so easy to make!

Answer: **constant**

DEVELOP

Choose the word on the right that is opposite in meaning to the word on the left. Circle the correct letter underneath the word.

1. **present**

there	absent	gift	give
A	B	C	D

2. **admit**

accuse	claim	deny	allow
A	B	C	D

3. **worst**

awful	better	off	best
A	B	C	D

4. **none**

all	some	null	empty
A	B	C	D

5. **blame**

award	praise	punish	cause
A	B	C	D

6. **lend**

give	steel	have	borrow
A	B	C	D

7. **junior**

kid	senior	child	adult
A	B	C	D

8. **heavy**

dark	shadow	light	dense
A	B	C	D

9. **strong**

off	weak	powerful	light
A	B	C	D

10. **hate**

love	loathe	like	fear
A	B	C	D

Check your answers at the back of the book before moving onto the timed test.

TIMED TEST 8

15:00
15 minutes

Select the word on the right from the given options which is opposite in meaning to the word on the left. Circle the correct letter underneath the word.

1.	**guest**	invited	party	hospitable	host
		A	B	C	D

2.	**curse**	spell	swear	bless	praise
		A	B	C	D

3.	**separate**	combine	part	mixture	mess
		A	B	C	D

4.	**cheerful**	grave	happy	smile	lonely
		A	B	C	D

5.	**closed**	ajar	shut	locked	wide
		A	B	C	D

6.	**supply**	require	demand	produce	give
		A	B	C	D

7.	**healthy**	keen	diseased	fit	inactive
		A	B	C	D

8.	**dawn**	dusk	twilight	midnight	noon
		A	B	C	D

9.	**rude**	bad	discourteous	polite	manners
		A	B	C	D

10.	**voluntary**	choice	help	compulsory	necessary
		A	B	C	D

11.	**external**	exterior	interior	internal	between
		A	B	C	D

12.	**odd**	strange	even	equal	likely
		A	B	C	D

13.	**brighten**	lighten	dark	fade	disappear
		A	B	C	D

14.	**powerful**	strong	weaker	feeble	massive
		A	B	C	D

15.	**wise**	clever	bright	foolish	careless
		A	B	C	D

16.	**fresh**	wind	stale	cold	clean
		A	B	C	D

17.	**seldom**	frequent	rare	nearly	never
		A	B	C	D

18.	**grow**	plant	tall	shrink	harvest
		A	B	C	D

19.	**valley**	dale	hill	precipice	river
		A	B	C	D

20.	**proud**	win	pride	weak	humble
		A	B	C	D

21.	**grant**	gift	refuse	ignore	help
		A	B	C	D

22.	**trivial**	notice	important	foolish	null
		A	B	C	D

| 23. | **intentional** | rule | purposeful | accidental | deliberate |
| | | A | B | C | D |

| 24. | **knowledge** | memory | forget | ignorance | unknown |
| | | A | B | C | D |

| 25. | **strict** | powerful | lenient | soft | hard |
| | | A | B | C | D |

| 26. | **boundless** | empty | endless | limited | closed |
| | | A | B | C | D |

| 27. | **lazy** | sleepy | alert | industrious | eloquent |
| | | A | B | C | E |

| 28. | **optimist** | pacifist | pessimist | hopeful | royalist |
| | | A | B | C | D |

| 29. | **poetry** | verse | song | prose | sentence |
| | | A | B | C | D |

| 30. | **wealth** | poverty | treasure | debt | power |
| | | A | B | C | D |

Remember to select an antonym rather than a synonym. Perhaps write 'opp' to stand for opposite down the margin a few times.

**THIS PAGE HAS DELIBERATELY
BEEN LEFT BLANK**

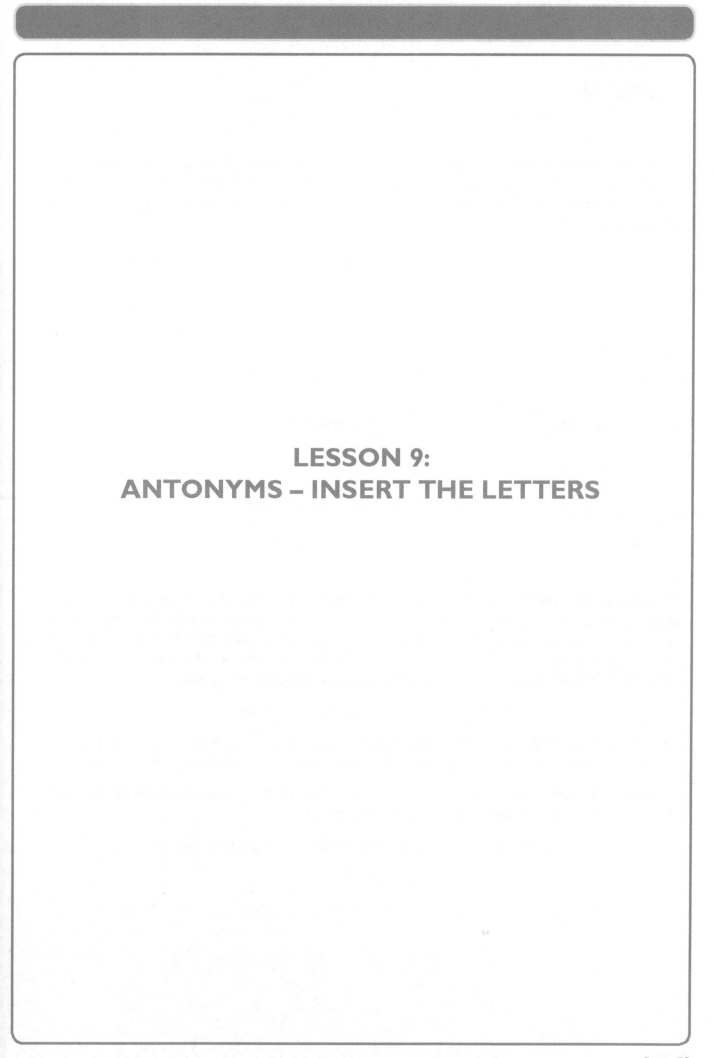

LESSON 9:
ANTONYMS – INSERT THE LETTERS

LEARN

Antonyms are words that are opposite in meaning. This popular Verbal Reasoning question type requires a good word knowledge and similar techniques to those used in the questions about synonyms. To help you start focusing on antonyms, rather than synonyms, try to think of as many opposite words as possible for the words below:

happy	create	small
wealthy	**complement**	**slender**

How did you get on? If you found this task challenging, you can always use a thesaurus or an antonyms/synonyms dictionary to help discover more opposite words. Remember, when answering these questions you must always select the same word class as the word on the left. For example, the word on the left below is **bellow** and this word is a verb. So, from the options, decide which word is a verb that means the opposite to bellow.

bellow whisper scream bawl quiet

The correct word from the list is *whisper* because it is an antonym and also a verb. *Bawl* and *scream* are verbs but also synonyms of *bellow*, while *quiet* is an adjective which rules it out too.

A useful tip to remember while tackling opposites is trying to spot useful prefixes. The prefixes *dis-*, *un-* or *in-* make a word an antonym. For example:

appear: disappear   healthy: unhealthy   expensive: inexpensive

Let's look at an example.

Complete the word on the right to spell a word that is an antonym of the word on the left.

certain   _ _ **ce** _ **t** _ _ **n**

Technique

1. Read the word on the left and think about its meaning and a possible antonym. Look at the incomplete word to see if the letters provided give a clue to the word needed.

2. Try to insert possible vowels or consonants which could belong in the spaces. This can also help identify the word. You may wish to consider whether a prefix could be added to the word on the left, which might also fit in the incomplete word.

3. Double check that the word is the opposite in meaning.

Answer: **uncertain**

When completing antonym questions, make sure the answers are opposite in meaning, not the closest!

DEVELOP

Complete the word on the right so it is opposite in meaning to the word on the left.

1. recommend   __ eje __ __

2. separate   __ __it __

3. acknowledge   i __ __ __ re

4. hasty   le__ __ __ __ ely

5. prohibit   au __ __ __ __ ise

6. wholesome   __ __h __ __ lthy

7. lament   cel __ __ __ __ te

8. obscure   __ __mou __

9. moderate   e __ __ __ eme

10. nimble   __ __um __ __

Check your answers at the back of the book before moving onto the timed test.

TIMED TEST 9

15:00
15 minutes

Complete the word on the right so it is opposite in meaning to the word on the left.

1. abandon   c __ __ __ m

2. complete   __ __f __ __ ish __ __

3. immediate   g __ __ du __ l

4. isolated   __ cce __ __ ible

5. success   __ ail __ __ __

6. probable   __ __ lik __ __ __

7. union   s __ __ arat __ __ __

8. turbulent   __ __ l __

9. hoax   o __ __ __ inal

10. observe   __ __ __ r __ gard

11. mellow   h __ __ s __

12. gregarious   res __ __ __ ed

13. inedible   pa __ at __ b __ __

14. interested   __ o __ __ d

15. just   __ __ f __ __ r

16. neat   di __ __ __ der __ y

17. objection   __ ppr __ __ al

18. traitor   p __ __ riot

19. wound   __ __ __ l

20. weary   __ n __r __ etic

21. trifle   pro __ __ __ nd

22. superior   __ __ f __ __ ior

23. stout   s __ __ __ der

24. imprisonment   fr __ __ d __ __

25. inaudible   __ o __ __

26. friend   __ o __

27. fatal   __ arm __ __ __ __

28. exterior   __ __ __ eri __ __

29. divine   __ ort __ __

30. dwindle   e __ p __ __ d

If you can't spot the answer instantly, look at the letters you've been given to see if you can see any likely spelling patterns.

LESSON 10:
VERBAL CLASSIFICATION

LEARN

This question type requires a knowledge of how to classify words and the ability to spot links between words. Making the connection between the words is the first stage. To help you identify these associations, write why the words below go together. Use this word bank to provide the clues.

> **jobs, colours, sports, computer parts, hats, joints, synonyms, young animals, trees, precious stones**

1. architect, chiropractor   _____

2. elbow, ankle   _____

3. beige, scarlet   _____

4. leveret, owlet   _____

5. sycamore, birch   _____

6. grave, solemn   _____

7. lacrosse, curling   _____

8. beret, fez   _____

9. topaz, sapphire   _____

10. keyboard, mouse   _____

Let's have a look at an example:

Select a word from the right that belongs with the group of words on the left in the best possible way.

jacket shirt jumper   trousers   socks   coat   shorts

A   B   C   D

Technique

1. Firstly, read all the words on the left and consider how they are classified. In the example above, it is clear they are all items of clothing.

2. The next step is to read the option answers and see how they could be associated to the three words on the left. As the words are also all items of clothing this doesn't help achieve the answer.

3. So, it is important to establish another link between the words on the left. The other common association is all the clothes are worn above the waist. Trousers, socks and shorts can now be eliminated.

4. Therefore, the correct answer is 'coat' option C.

Answer: **coat**

DEVELOP

Select a word from the right that belongs with the group of words on the left in the best possible way. Circle the correct letter underneath the word.

1. chair, bench, stool

table	throne	shelf	chest
A	B	C	D

2. eye, nose, mouth

arm	ear	leg	smile
A	B	C	D

3. breeze, gale, wind

sleet	wave	hurricane	cloud
A	B	C	D

4. Monday, Tuesday, Friday

winter	Saturday	Sunday	Thursday
A	B	C	D

5. swede, potato, parsnip

pea	apple	vegetable	carrot
A	B	C	D

6. aunt, sister, mother

cousin	brother	family	niece
A	B	C	D

7. cold, chilly, icy

hot	cool	temperature	radiator
A	B	C	D

8. run, sprint, jog

walk	stroll	dash	wander
A	B	C	D

9. wheel, handlebar, pedal

chain	exhaust	seatbelt	cushion
A	B	C	D

10. orange, yellow, green

paint	colour	pale	crimson
A	B	C	D

Check your answers at the back of the book before moving onto the timed test.

TIMED TEST 10

`15:00` 15 minutes

Select a word from the right that belongs with the group of words on the left in the best possible way. Circle the correct letter underneath the word.

1. son, boy, male

lass	lad	girl	maid
A	B	C	D

2. vexed, angry, cross

cry	moan	furious	mood
A	B	C	D

3. cream, butter, cheese

water	yoghurt	egg	flour
A	B	C	D

4. cylinder, sphere, cuboid

hexagon	oval	cone	kite
A	B	C	D

5. maid, girl, lass

mother	wife	maiden	grandma
A	B	C	D

6. tap, knock, boot

kick	slipper	shoe	sandal
A	B	C	D

7. infant, child, tot

boy	baby	girl	daughter
A	B	C	D

8. voyage, journey, expedition

trek	break	travel	distance
A	B	C	D

9. feast, repast, snack

festival	famine	food	meal
A	B	C	D

10. three, eleven, nine

thirty	seven	twenty	eight
A	B	C	D

		A	B	C	D
11.	Italy, France, Germany	Britain	Spain	Iceland	Ireland
12.	doe, cow, mare	foal	cub	sow	calf
13.	crab, crayfish, prawn	mackerel	lobster	jellyfish	herring
14.	Mars, Venus, Jupiter	Saturn	comet	Moon	star
15.	Paris, Rome, Washington	Sydney	London	New York	Barcelona
16.	crown, throne, orb	royalty	reign	succession	sceptre
17.	custom, rule, practice	equip	habit	supply	dress
18.	salamander, newt, frog	snake	toad	lizard	snail
19.	holly, cedar, spruce	willow	pine	sycamore	beech
20.	snowflake, icicle, iceberg	lake	raindrop	glacier	waterfall

21.	parsley, sage, rosemary	raspberry	lime	onion	thyme
		A	B	C	D

22.	jacket, coat, cape	suit	sweatshirt	blouse	anorak
		A	B	C	D

23.	fur, hair, hide	seek	fleece	plait	tangle
		A	B	C	D

24.	polish, varnish, laminate	veneer	slice	scratch	plastic
		A	B	C	D

25.	June, July, August	Monday	month	December	summer
		A	B	C	D

26.	two, five, seventeen	eleven	nine	twenty-one	six
		A	B	C	D

27.	silk, wool, cotton	nylon	linen	polyester	viscose
		A	B	C	D

28.	shark, ray, swordfish	dolphin	whale	porpoise	piranha
		A	B	C	D

29.	hostel, inn, motel	priory	lodge	restaurant	cafeteria
		A	B	C	D

30.	Tudor, Plantagenet, Windsor	London	Victoria	Stuart	Charles
		A	B	C	D

THIS PAGE HAS DELIBERATELY BEEN LEFT BLANK

SECTION 2:
MAKE YOUR OWN GLOSSARY
AND ANSWERS

MAKE YOUR OWN GLOSSARY

Record any unfamiliar words below and write a concise definition. Remember to revise this list nearer to your exam dates.

Word	Definition

Answers

Lesson 1 answers: Odd one out

Develop: Odd one out (page 8)

	Answer		Explanation
1.	D	interested	The other words all mean kind.
2.	C	cousin	A cousin is not always female, but all the others are female family members.
3.	B	report	All the others are forms of fictional writing.
4.	D	beast	The others are all synonyms for ghost.
5.	A	twinkle	All the others are steady forms of light.
6.	D	robin	The others are birds of prey.
7.	A	stranger	All the others are types of friend.
8.	B	middle	The other words are used to refer to an edge.
9.	C	trousers	All the others are words that also mean dress.
10.	D	peas	All the other vegetables grow underground.

Timed test 1: Odd one out (page 9)

	Answer		Explanation
1.	D	donor	All the others mean a bad person.
2.	D	confusing	All the other words mean careless.
3.	C	erratic	All the others mean stable and unchanging.
4.	A	pine	The others are all deciduous trees.
5.	C	Scotland	The other three places are islands.
6.	B	sage	All the others are religious leaders.
7.	D	shallot	The others are all fruits.
8.	A	waddle	The rest are types of penguin.
9.	B	agreement	All the other words describe ill-mannered ways of speaking.
10.	B	Dalmatian	The others are breeds of cat.
11.	C	somewhat	All the other words mean completely.
12.	C	mobile	The other words mean of bad intent.
13.	A	sever	The other three all mean extremely serious or urgent, but sever means to cut.
14.	D	letter	The others are ways of speaking.
15.	C	force	All the others mean to give way or give in.
16.	B	scene	The others are all words for something that has happened.
17.	D	hoard	All the others describe a noisy commotion.
18.	B	responsible	The others are ways to describe a friendly person.
19.	C	particular	The other words mean maybe.
20.	C	insane	All the other words mean eccentric too.

Answers

21.	A	intelligible	The others are all words to describe something that is difficult to explain.
22.	C	distant	The others mean that something is about to happen.
23.	C	favour	The others refer to types of magic spell.
24.	A	plastic	The others are all ways of looking at things.
25.	B	music	The others describe someone's behaviour.
26.	C	disconcerted	The rest are ways to describe groups of people in confusion.
27.	B	bulbous	All the others are synonyms for exaggerated.
28.	C	efficacious	The other words mean ineffective.
29.	C	hat	The others describe a dull or dark place.
30.	A	circuit	All the others mean join together.

Lesson 2 answers: Odd two out

Develop: Odd two out (page 13)

	Answer	Explanation
1.	A hands C horse	The others are intervals of time.
2.	A thought D because	The others are prepositions.
3.	A mauve D violet	The others are shades of pink.
4.	A cheese D butter	All the others are meat but these are dairy.
5.	A relax D rest	The others refer to temperature.
6.	D cousin E sibling	The others are all male members of the family, while cousin and sibling could be male or female.
7.	C shed E garage	The rest are rooms inside the house.
8.	B butterfly C bumblebee	The other creatures do not fly.
9.	C expire E lapse	The other words mean to encourage.
10.	B abhor D dislike	These words mean to hate something but the others mean to like.

Answers

Timed test 2: Odd two out (page 14)

	Answer	Explanation
1.	B potato D carrot	All the others are vegetables with leaves and grow above ground.
2.	D library E newsagent	All the others are things you read.
3.	C door E floor	The others are all floor coverings.
4.	B lemon C mint	The others are flowers.
5.	A shock E aboard	All the other words mean to begin.
6.	B strength D cheerful	The others are shellfish.
7.	A emu C penguin	The other birds can fly.
8.	D camp E holiday	All the others refer to types of journeys with a purpose.
9.	C secret D treasure	The others mean being beneath the earth.
10.	B inject E expect	The others are all methods of removing something.
11.	B converse D concede	All the others mean to end.
12.	A gap C hole	The others are verbs meaning to make a hole in something.
13.	A flourish B disappear	All the other words mean to become shrunken.
14.	D happy E table	All the other words can be verbs.
15.	A child E person	The other words relate to friendship.
16.	A great B good	All the others are parts of a fireplace.
17.	D intruding E ingrowing	The others mean sticking out.
18.	D bramble E marathon	The others are all types of walk.
19.	A whisper C instruct	All the others are types of public speaking.
20.	B mint D sage	The others are all flowers.

Answers

21.	D greed E jealousy	The others refer to virtuous feelings.
22.	A fox E artwork	All the other words are synonyms for sly.
23.	B foal D bullock	All the others are female animals, but these are young animals.
24.	A abandon E building	All the others are words for home.
25.	D steady E sedate	The others are all synonyms for fast.
26.	B baton E race	All the others are synonyms for broadcast.
27.	B block D paper	All the others are a small part broken off something bigger.
28.	C think E look	The other words are palindromes (that is they spell the same word backwards too).
29.	B idol E speedy	All the others mean lazy or slow.
30.	B fire C dragon	The other words mean to put an end to something.

Lesson 3 answers: Reshuffled sentences

Develop: Reshuffled sentences (page 20)

	Answer	Sentence
1.	court	She/he cooked the fish after she/he caught it.
2.	hurting	Nobody likes to hurt somebody else.
3.	door	The new house is very close by.
4.	quaking	I heard a chorus of quacking ducks.
5.	strike	We won the match quite easily.
6.	is	Yesterday it was such fun for everyone.
7.	was	He has gone shopping for his mother's birthday present.
8.	far	Move closer so I can see you.
9.	determine	He was intent on doing well.
10.	behind	You must follow the regulations precisely.

Answers

Timed test 3: Reshuffled sentences (page 21)

	Answer	Explanation
1.	umbrella	She is feeling under the weather today.
2.	as	I think we should continue with our plans.
3.	know	I don't think of myself as stupid.
4.	honest	Is there really a need for that?
5.	plane	We are due to fly at dusk.
6.	in	He is not invited on special occasions.
7.	hand	He held her in great esteem.
8.	difficulty	The journey is a long and arduous one.
9.	during	It was extremely cold in the library.
10.	going	Do not run when you are crossing the road.
11.	clown	Everyone burst out laughing when they saw him.
12.	because	We enjoyed the walk despite the rain.
13.	snuggles	James climbed the stairs and got into bed.
14.	arrive	We visited the museum on a Saturday afternoon.
15.	they	I am concerned that he might hurt himself.
16.	mirror	Every morning I brush/shampoo and shampoo/brush my hair.
17.	it	I don't quite understand your problem.
18.	unable	We are not going to succeed without a plan.
19.	scissors	He made a very cutting remark.
20.	right	She left her shoes by mistake.
21.	day	Every week I go dancing on a Thursday.
22.	down	I was looking forward to having a wonderful time.
23.	speed	The quick dog raced after the stick.
24.	agent	The secret mission was accomplished successfully.
25.	choose	Unfortunately my first preference was not available.
26.	down	I think I know where the problem lies.
27.	led	The extreme winter temperatures caused disruption to services.
28.	repaired	Dad ought to be able to fix it.
29.	famous	He was extremely skilled at swerving the ball.
30.	slope	He was inclined not to answer.

Answers

Lesson 4 answers: Analogies

Develop: Analogies (page 26)

	Answer	Explanation
1.	cat, dog	These are the adult names for their infants.
2.	book, window	These are things that can be made from the two materials.
3.	liquid, solid	These are the states of matter for water and ice.
4.	rails, road	This gives the track along which each vehicle moves.
5.	feet, hands	This is the body part used for each action.
6.	honesty, deceit	Here you have synonyms for each word.
7.	smile, frown	These are facial expressions related to each emotion.
8.	laces, belt	This gives the manner by which each item is secured.
9.	eyes, ears	This is the part of the body related to each sense.
10.	sugar, salt	The flavour attributable to each foodstuff.

Timed test 4: Analogies (page 27)

	Answer	Explanation
1.	confined, spacious	These adjectives describe each type of space.
2.	empty, fill	These verbs are synonyms.
3.	cheerful, despondent	These are synonyms for each word.
4.	famous, unknown	These adjectives are synonyms.
5.	sponge, rubber	Here you have examples of materials with each quality.
6.	deny, binge	These are synonyms for each word.
7.	sick, healthy	These adjectives describe the look of someone in each state of health.
8.	contradiction, confirmation	These are synonyms for each word.
9.	unproductive, fruitful	These adjectives are synonyms.
10.	annoy, value	These words describe each sentiment.
11.	expert, graduate	A novice becomes an expert and a freshman becomes a graduate if they each complete their training.
12.	stone, pip	This is the seed in the middle of each fruit.
13.	wealth, poverty	These are relative states of affluence for each social rank.
14.	cheep, quack	This is the noise made by each creature.
15.	impromptu, rehearsed	There are words that describe each level of readiness.
16.	boar, elephant	This is the type of nose that each animal has.
17.	bizarre, ordinary	These are synonyms for each word.
18.	hare, kangaroo	These are larger 'cousins' of each animal.

Answers

19.	ankle, wrist	This is the joint at the end of each body part.
20.	horse, snake	This is the way these animals move about.
21.	eel, possum	These are the adult of each young animal.
22.	twenty-five, four	This is the square of each number.
23.	coal, beer	This is the product of each job type.
24.	painter, sculptor	This artist creates each type of work.
25.	raw, trams	Each word is spelt backwards.
26.	music, ideas	This is what the person doing each job produces.
27.	eight, four	Each number is divided by six.
28.	stink, warts	Each word is spelt backwards.
29.	fawn, squab	This is the name for each animal's young.
30.	space, weather	The area of interest for each type of scientist is given.

Lesson 5 answers: Multiple meanings

Develop: Multiple meanings (page 32)

	Answer	Word			Answer	Word
1.	E	date		6.	B	rose
2.	B	leaves		7.	D	bow
3.	A	point		8.	C	wound
4.	C	right		9.	A	minute
5.	D	type		10.	E	sewer

Timed test 5: Multiple meanings (page 34)

	Answer	Word			Answer	Word
1.	C	bear		16.	D	pound
2.	C	ring		17.	A	fit
3.	E	bat		18.	C	row
4.	B	sole		19.	A	space
5.	D	bright		20.	C	train
6.	C	fine		21.	B	well
7.	E	peer		22.	D	desert
8.	D	ground		23.	A	tear
9.	A	kind		24.	C	fair
10.	C	wind		25.	D	left
11.	A	light		26.	A	mine
12.	C	match		27.	B	log
13.	B	clip		28.	D	bore
14.	C	barge		29.	C	stall
15.	E	bark		30.	B	wave

Answers

Lesson 6 answers: Matching synonyms

Develop: Matching synonyms (page 42)

	Answer	Word
1.	A	scribble
2.	C	pleased
3.	A	throw
4.	D	brag
5.	B	mill

	Answer	Word
6.	A	retort
7.	B	expand
8.	D	examine
9.	C	learner
10.	C	definitely

Timed test 6: Matching synonyms (page 43)

	Answer	Word
1.	B	icon
2.	C	design
3.	B	stout
4.	A	restore
5.	B	weep
6.	D	reservoir
7.	B	optimistic
8.	D	sturdy
9.	C	ample
10.	A	plead
11.	A	trek
12.	C	bare
13.	A	chortle
14.	D	crafty
15.	B	referee

	Answer	Word
16.	B	impartial
17.	C	mammoth
18.	A	push
19.	D	reveal
20.	B	depression
21.	C	chum
22.	D	pew
23.	B	edit
24.	A	halt
25.	C	trespass
26.	D	compulsory
27.	A	idea
28.	B	aligned
29.	D	operative
30.	D	hanker

Lesson 7 answers: Synonyms – insert the letters

Develop: Synonyms – insert the letters (page 48)

	Answer
1.	scream
2.	talented
3.	cabinet
4.	drizzle
5.	spin

	Answer
6.	mouldy
7.	correct
8.	stroll
9.	dislike
10.	twilight

Timed test 7: Synonyms – insert the letters (page 49)

	Answer
1.	enough
2.	ecstatic
3.	profession
4.	extravagant
5.	momentary
6.	attractive
7.	careless
8.	humble
9.	perilous
10.	flimsy
11.	boring
12.	ridicule
13.	crooked
14.	gullible
15.	enlarge

	Answer
16.	amount
17.	describe
18.	unnamed
19.	leaflet
20.	entice
21.	peaceful
22.	courage
23.	sizeable
24.	raise
25.	license/licence
26.	delicious
27.	compliment
28.	gathering
29.	uninterested
30.	business

Answers

Lesson 8 answers: Matching antonyms

Develop: Matching antonyms (page 54)

	Answer	
1.	B	absent
2.	C	deny
3.	D	best
4.	A	all
5.	B	praise

	Answer	
6.	D	borrow
7.	B	senior
8.	C	light
9.	B	weak
10.	A	love

Timed Test 8: Matching antonyms (page 55)

	Answer	
1.	D	host
2.	C	bless
3.	A	combine
4.	A	grave
5.	A	ajar
6.	B	demand
7.	B	diseased
8.	A	dusk
9.	C	polite
10.	C	compulsory
11.	C	internal
12.	B	even
13.	C	fade
14.	C	feeble
15.	C	foolish

	Answer	
16.	B	stale
17.	A	frequent
18.	C	shrink
19.	B	hill
20.	D	humble
21.	B	refuse
22.	B	important
23.	C	accidental
24.	C	ignorance
25.	B	lenient
26.	C	limited
27.	C	industrious
28.	B	pessimist
29.	C	prose
30.	A	poverty

Lesson 9 answers: Antonyms – insert the letters

Develop: Antonyms – insert the letters (page 62)

	Answer
1.	reject
2.	unite
3.	ignore
4.	leisurely
5.	authorise

	Answer
6.	unhealthy
7.	celebrate
8.	famous
9.	extreme
10.	clumsy

Answers

Timed Test 9: Antonyms – insert the letters (page 63)

	Answer			Answer
1.	claim		16.	disorderly
2.	unfinished		17.	approval
3.	gradual		18.	patriot
4.	accessible		19.	heal
5.	failure		20.	energetic
6.	unlikely		21.	profound
7.	separation		22.	inferior
8.	calm		23.	slender
9.	original		24.	freedom
10.	disregard		25.	loud
11.	harsh		26.	foe
12.	reserved		27.	harmless
13.	palatable		28.	interior
14.	bored		29.	mortal
15.	unfair		30.	expand

Lesson 10 answers: Verbal classification

Develop: Verbal classification (page 68)

	Letter	Answer	Explanation
1.	B	throne	All are pieces of furniture for sitting on.
2.	B	ear	All are body parts positioned on the head.
3.	C	hurricane	All are types of wind.
4.	D	Thursday	All are weekdays.
5.	D	carrot	All are vegetables that grow under the ground.
6.	D	niece	All are female relatives.
7.	B	cool	All are synonyms for cold.
8.	C	dash	All are synonyms for run.
9.	A	chain	All are parts of a bicycle.
10.	D	crimson	All are colours.

Answers

Timed test 10: Verbal classification (page 69)

	Letter	Answer	Explanation
1.	B	lad	All are masculine nouns.
2.	C	furious	All are synonyms for angry.
3.	B	yoghurt	All are milk products.
4.	C	cone	All have curved faces.
5.	C	maiden	All are synonyms for a young female.
6.	A	kick	All are verbs to do with hitting.
7.	B	baby	All are names for a young child.
8.	A	trek	All are types of journey.
9.	D	meal	All are occasions when food is eaten.
10.	B	seven	All are odd numbers.
11.	B	Spain	All are countries on mainland Europe.
12.	C	sow	All are names for female animals.
13.	B	lobster	All have shells.
14.	A	Saturn	All are planets.
15.	B	London	All are capital cities.
16.	D	sceptre	All are concrete nouns relating to royalty.
17.	B	habit	All these words are a normal way of behaving.
18.	B	toad	All are amphibians
19.	B	pine	All are evergreen trees.
20.	C	glacier	All are frozen water.
21.	D	thyme	All are herbs.
22.	D	anorak	All are types of outer garment.
23.	B	fleece	All are coats of different animals.
24.	A	veneer	All are different types of wood surface.
25.	C	December	All are months of the year.
26.	A	eleven	All are prime numbers.
27.	B	linen	All are natural fibres (the others are manufactured).
28.	D	piranha	All are types of fish.
29.	B	lodge	All are places to stay in.
30.	C	Stuart	All are dynasties of the Royal Family through the ages.

Well done; now see how you did on the marking chart on the next page.

Marking Chart

Fill in the tables below with your results from each test. Each test is out of 30.

Odd one out	/30		Matching synonyms	/30
Odd two out	/30		Synonyms – insert the letters	/30
Reshuffled sentences	/30		Matching antonyms	/30
Analogies	/30		Antonyms – insert the letters	/30
Multiple meanings	/30		Verbal classification	/30
Total Score				/300

Progress Grid

Colour the chart below with your total mark from each lesson to see how well you have done.

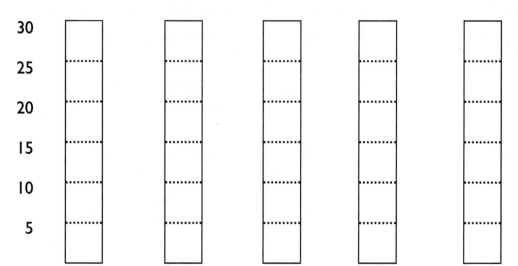

Odd one out Odd two out Reshuffled sentences Analogies Multiple meanings

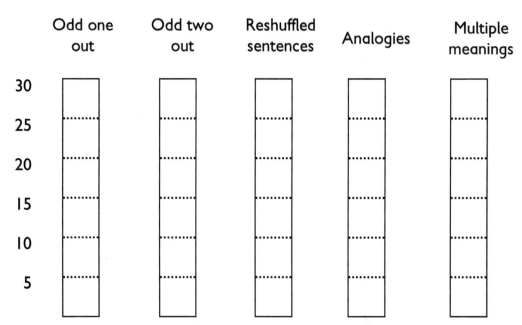

Matching synonyms Synomyms – insert the letters Matching antomyms Antonyms – insert the letters Verbal classification

Read the statements below for some hints and tips.

Below 10:   Re-read the technique section and have another go at the Develop questions.

10–20   Good effort. Retry some of the questions that you got wrong.

20–25   Well done. Keep enhancing your skills.

25 +   You're a star. Keep up the hard work.